POETIC VOYAGES
MAIDENHEAD

Edited by Lucy Jeacock

First published in Great Britain in 2001 by
YOUNG WRITERS
Remus House,
Coltsfoot Drive,
Peterborough, PE2 9JX
Telephone (01733) 890066

HB ISBN 0 75433 238 1
SB ISBN 0 75433 239 X

FOREWORD

Young Writers was established in 1991 with the aim to promote creative writing in children, to make reading and writing poetry fun.

This year once again, proved to be a tremendous success with over 88,000 entries received nationwide.

The Poetic Voyages competition has shown us the high standard of work and effort that children are capable of today. It is a reflection of the teaching skills in schools, the enthusiasm and creativity they have injected into their pupils shines clearly within this anthology.

The task of selecting poems was therefore a difficult one but nevertheless, an enjoyable experience. We hope you are as pleased with the final selection in *Poetic Voyages Maidenhead* as we are.

CONTENTS

Gurpreet Bharya	72
Harriet Pridmore	74
Annie Godfrey	75
Stephanie Rowan	76
Nathacia-Mary Sikkel	77
Catherine Sayer	78
Gemma Bartholomew	79
Linda Parker	80
Ross Pepper	81
Leila Gilhooly	82
Hannah Evans	83
Emmy Alghabra	84
Rachel Mercy	85
Eleanor Fricker	86
Sophie Lyons	87
Ben Stuart	88
Elli Thatcher Jones	89
Holly Bennett	90
Katie Alston	91
Erif Newman	92
Bryony Holt	93
Georgina Fidler	94
Louise Rayfield	95
Kelly-Anne Chivers	96
Cara Guest	97
Linda Third	98
Lucie Lapham	99
Rachel Ashe	100
Kristina Butler	101
Sarah Wilson	102
Harriet Burdett	103
Bianca Heath	104
Julia Walton	105

Ellington Primary School
Imran Hussain	106
Rizwana Mahmood	107
Valerie Kondo	108

Furze Platt Junior School

Michael Kirton	109
Sam Carter	110
Juliet Clark	111
Siân Osborn	112
Christopher Watts	113
Isobelle Vernon-Smith	114
Stuart Shepherd	115
Ryan Simmonds	116
Jessica Whitworth	117
James Cawthorpe	118
Nicola Courtier	119
Rachel Christian	120
Ryan Jones	121
Robert Ashburner	122
Malcolm Gledhill	123
Kirsty Arena	124
Erik Williams	125
Amelia Hendry	126
Tom Watts	127
Hannah Heales	128
Fleur Hughes	129
Jake Leonard	130
Georgina Kirkwood	131
Daniel Love	132
Lucy Higgon	133
Heidi Goldsmith	134
Nicola Skidmore	135
Laura Hay	136
Colin Cooper	137
Morgan Smith	138
Abigail Giles	139
Thomas Hopkins	140
Tim Armstrong	141
Sam Langford	142
Amelia Hilsdon	143
Thomas Davies	144
Grace Grimmett	145

The Poems

Is It A Dream?

Beware of the night,
No people are in sight,
You go for an evening stroll,
Where you find an almighty fright.
You see little shapes turn into monsters . . .
And then disappear out of sight.

Jamie Lucas (9)
Cookham Rise Primary School

LEE

There once was a boy called Lee
Who was making a cup of tea
He fell off his chair
And gave a glare
Because he cut his knee.

Amy Welberry (8)
Cookham Rise Primary School

THE BIN ALIEN

Watch out for the bin alien,
Who lurks in his dingy bin,
Waiting for an unprepared passer-by,
To leap on and perform a sin.

Nobody knows where he's from,
Mars, Jupiter, Neptune, Pluto,
How did he get here?
Extraterrestrial ship, space shuttle, UFO.

His hands can grab you,
His eyes can melt you,
His teeth can mash you,
This monster has no limits of things he can do.

Julian Morlet (8)
Cookham Rise Primary School

THE LION

Fierce and brave
He hunts like a king
Stronger than a bear
Lazy like a fat man sleeping
The king of animals
A meat eating cat
He owns the jungle.

Janghir Summandar (9)
Cookham Rise Primary School

AUTUMN

Autumn when the light breeze blows,
golden leaves fall down below.
All the trees are tall and bare,
stand so still without a care.

Hedgehogs burrow in the leaves,
bunnies play in the breeze.
Squirrels gather nuts with mothers,
foxes stay safe, under covers.

Nuts and berries are all to spare,
apples, oranges and a single pear.
Sticks and hay to build their dens,
keeps creatures warm to winter's end.

Leaves and trees all look dead,
animals have hibernated in their beds.
The countryside is cold and bare,
look! Winter over there.

Matthew Brayne (9)
Cookham Rise Primary School

JUNGLE BUNGLE

Down in the jungle
Lions roar
Monkeys laugh
When they are bored.

Frogs are happy
When they jump
But when lions roar
Their throats get a lump.

Snakes slither
Round and round
They wish they could fly
But they stay on the ground.

Crocodiles swim about
Snapping for their food
Be careful at dinner time
He might be in a mood!

Emily Ponter (8)
Cookham Rise Primary School

THE HAIRY PIG

You should be scared of the hairy pig
That everybody hates
Or he'll take you to his scary house
And put you on his plate
His teeth are sharp
His house is dark
He'll eat you like a shark
His blood is black and boiling hot
His breath is smelly too
He hates people . . .
Especially you!

Daniel Coulson (9)
Cookham Rise Primary School

ROLY

I've got a dog called Roly,
And he is just so scruffy!
But when he has a bath,
He suddenly turns fluffy!

Roly loves to play,
He loves to play with his ball,
But sometimes the ball goes just too fast . . .
And he skids into the wall.

I love my dog called Roly,
He is just so mad!
But sometimes we have to tell him off,
Because he has been bad!

Amy Clark (9)
Cookham Rise Primary School

THERE'S A MONSTER UNDER MY BED!

There's a monster under my bed
And he looks kinda scary
He has an enormous, ugly head
And a body that's green and hairy.

He sleeps right through the whole day
And wakes up in the night
You shouldn't wake him up in any way
Or he'll give you a *fright!*

He has mystical powers to mess up my room
And I always get the blame
He disappears with a big *boom!*
As if it's some kind of game.

Laura Pidgley (9)
Cookham Rise Primary School

MOBILES

Mobiles are pretty things,
they hang from the ceiling
and shine in the sun.

Mobiles are pretty things
they come in all shapes
and sizes.

Mobiles are pretty things
they hang around all day long
and twist and turn in the wind.

Mobiles are pretty things
they chime outside all the time
and twinkle in the sun.

Mobiles are pretty things
they look like animals
and sometimes like fruit.

Mobiles are pretty things
they make a room look bright
and cheer you up when you are feeling down.

Mobiles are pretty things
they hang about talking to one another
and fall asleep at night.

Stephanie Wright (9)
Cookham Rise Primary School

THE SPIDER

Have you seen the spider
Crawling up the wall?
Evil is its eye
Looking for a fly.

Have you seen the spider
Lurking in the bath?
Gripping on with his eight legs
It will never fall.

Have you seen the spider
In the middle of its web?
Black and hairy
Oh so scary
Touch him if you dare!

Andrew Knox (9)
Cookham Rise Primary School

FOOTBALL MATCH

Whistle blows
Ball rolls
Fast running up the pitch
Crunching tackle
Crowd roars
Super save
And finally a
Goal!

George Bond (9)
Cookham Rise Primary School

RAIN

Trickling down the windows
Pouring down the gutters
Splattering on the patio
Dripping off the trees
We need the rain
But please, please stop
I want to play outside!

Matthew Taylor (8)
Cookham Rise Primary School

TWO LITTLE KITTENS

Two little kittens, sitting in a tree,
Would they like to play with me?
One is ginger, one is grey,
Will they play with me today?
I tickle their tummies and stroke their fur,
They love it so much they begin to purr,
When they look tired I'll put them to bed
And that's where they'll stay till it's time to be fed.

Vicky Woodhams (7)
Cookham Rise Primary School

FOOTBALL

Football is a team sport,
I play it when I can,
Sometimes played by women,
Often played by man.

Eleven players in a team,
Two teams have to play,
90 minutes for each match,
45 minutes each way.

The idea is to kick the ball,
And then hopefully you will score,
Run up and down the pitch again,
Then maybe score some more!

James Woodhams (7)
Cookham Rise Primary School

I MAY NOT

I may not be a cook
But I can bake a cake

I have not climbed a ladder
But I can walk upstairs

I may not have rode a boat
But I have been in the sea

I may not have a lot of friends
But I love my sisters a lot

I may not be a poet
But I try my best at stories.

Jocelyn Ducellier (7)
Cookham Rise Primary School

My Mum

My mum
is a pretty kind of mum
She loves eating chocolate
She goes shopping all the time
Shop till you drop
My mum will take you anywhere
My mum is a hippy chick
She's wacky
She's wonderful
My mum is always putting make-up on
to look beautiful
I really love my mum
She always has a good long gossip
about looks and make-up on the phone
She will always give you a good time.

Isabelle Jane Bradley (7)
Cookham Rise Primary School

DAISY'S BUSY WEEK

There once lived a little dog
Her name was Daisy.

Monday was special
It was her 2nd birthday.
Daisy had many gifts
A bone, her favourite, she sniffed.

On Wednesday she went for a run.
She met a friendly dog
And had lots of fun.

They went back to Daisy's
And had a yummy tea.
Daisy thought 'He's great, he's the one for me!'

Friday was special
It was her wedding day.
Daisy married the friendly dog
His name was Ray.

Rebecca Holly Davies (7)
Cookham Rise Primary School

RUN, RUN, RUN!

Out late at night is the fox
Under the stars, in the moonlight
Red bushy tail, white little socks
Hunting for his dinner tonight
Dawn has broken, sun will be rising
Hunters coming with their red jackets and sacks
Guns will be shooting and hounds howling
Run, run, run, escape from the packs.

Jordan Pleace (8)
Cookham Rise Primary School

My Imaginary Chinese Dragon

Last night I was dreaming about a Chinese dragon,
To be honest he wasn't frightening.
He was kind and always had something on his mind,
Always had something boring like sleeping and snoring.
He was wearing my hat and sitting on my *best* mat!
Me and my dragon became best friends,
But the saddest thing about it was that it was only a dream.

Catherine Gauld (7)
Cookham Rise Primary School

AT THE FUNFAIR

Burgers and donuts,
waltzers, swing boats, rockets
all the things I love.
The funfair came to town last week,
I went with all my friends.
We went on the octopus and ghost train.
Me and my friends won a goldfish each,
there were lots of prizes to win.
We tried to win some sweets at the shooting gallery,
we didn't win anything.
But we had a fabulous time.

James Straw (8)
Cookham Rise Primary School

ALL SEASONS

In autumn there is a swirling breeze
In spring the blossom makes me sneeze

In summer the birds fly high in the trees
Far above the buzzing bees

But in winter Jack Frost can bite
And the howling weather keeps me awake at night

Which is my favourite season?
I cannot say!
Each has its own appeal
Depending on its day.

Matthew Earl (8)
Cookham Rise Primary School

THE SNOWMAN

On one winter's morning
It began to snow
It snowed, it snowed
It snowed, it snowed
Me and my friends
Decided to build a snowman
We made a little ball
Which grew and grew
I shouted 'We need two'
We put them on top of each other
He was as tall as my brother
Bert got a carrot for his nose
Where from, nobody knows
I put my scarf around his neck
And found some stones for his eyes
They were quite big like mince pies
He was quite round
As he stood on the ground
The sun came out and he grinned
As he started melting
After a while he was gone
Disappearing to water
Goodbye snowman we said.

Scott Andrews (9)
Cookham Rise Primary School

THE SWIMMING POOL

Swimming, swimming, swimming in a pool,
in a big hall it is better than being at school.

Swimming in a pool is fun and cool,
you can have a dive and it brings you alive.

One side is shallow and the other is deep,
you can leap and splash in a pool.

There is a slide and it is fast
and I landed with a splash.
I didn't know how fast it was,
I thought I would crash.

Joanna Hopes (9)
Cookham Rise Primary School

PADDI

I have got a little sister,
her name is Paddi.
She's got brown hair
and she will do anything for a dare.

She's three year's old
and she's as good as gold.
She eats lots of sweets
but doesn't like brushing her teeth.

At six o'clock she has a bath,
my sister is definitely not daft.
She does her homework every night
and doesn't let the bed bugs bite.

Amber Wetherall (10)
Cookham Rise Primary School

THE ORCHESTRA

The percussion is
Keeping the beat
With their feet.

The woodwind plays
High and low
As they blow.

The brass goes
Up with a toot
And down with a hoot.

The strings keep
Up with the flow
By moving the bow.

Above them all, in the stand
Is the man with the magic hand.

The orchestra performs
Boom, bang, whistle, twang,
Toot, hoot, strum, clang.

Laurence Sparkes (9)
Cookham Rise Primary School

BIKES

When I'm on my bike,
I can do anything I like.

I feel the wind in my hair,
I haven't a care.

I'm flying to Mars,
As I zoom past cars.

It's what I like to do,
When I hear cows moo.

Round the corners I go,
Round the corners I slow.

Everything is great,
As I go through the gate.

I want some more,
As I go through the door.

I can do anything I like,
When I'm on my *bike!*

Danielle Norman (10)
Cookham Rise Primary School

I WISH . . .

I wish I were a F1 driver
Roaring round the roadway
I wish I could eat scrumptious chocolate
And not have to pay

I wish I could play for Arsenal
And hear the crowd sing
I wish my mum would clear up for me
In the speed you could say bing!

I wish I could play on the PlayStation
And not wait my turn
I wish I could buy all the toys I want
And not have to earn!

I wish I never ever got told off
And I was always in the right
I wish I didn't have to go to school
But, still be very bright!

I wish I could have a dog
His name would be Rrrroger!
I wish for 'Roller Coaster Tycoon'
To build a ride called 'Dodger'

I wish all these wishes would come true
And not have to wait in a queue!

Andrew Davies (10)
Cookham Rise Primary School

THE FAIRGROUND

'Where are we going Mum?'
'We're going on an outing.'
Drove off in the car
And heard music and shouting.

We could smell hot dogs
As we got nearer
Saw a big wheel
It got clearer and clearer.

We parked the car
And then got out
Started running
To the roundabout.

We got off the ride
And felt quite dizzy
Over to the chairoplane
It was very, very busy.

Kieron Middleditch (10)
Cookham Rise Primary School

CATS

Cats are fluffy
Kittens are too
I love cats
Mind your cats don't get the flu.

Do not tease them
Treat them well
Get them some food
Collar, tag and bell.

Vets may be needed
From time to time
To keep your cat healthy
Mistreating is a crime.

Louise Isted (9)
Cookham Rise Primary School

SUMMER

Summer's nice and hot,
So don't get in a knot.
Put some ice in your drink,
To cool your brain and make you think.
Jolly song of the ice-cream man,
The cooling breeze of a nice, cool fan.
Swimming in a swimming pool,
Making sure you're nice 'n' cool.
Don't get sunburnt,
That'll be a lesson learnt.
Always sticky in the night,
Under the moonlight.

Jade Francis (9)
Cookham Rise Primary School

ANIMALS

Some animals are scary,
Some animals are sweet,
I like dolphins,
Birds always tweet.

Some animals live in forests,
I like foxes,
Some animals are home ones,
Some get dumped in boxes.

Some are very big,
Some are very small,
Some are very thin,
Some are very tall.

Dogs are nice,
What about a cat,
Look after all animals,
Some animals sit on mats.

Eleanor Gay (10)
Cookham Rise Primary School

STORMS

Storms usually come in the night,
They really give you quite a fright.

People think it's just rain,
Some get frightened out of their brain,
As thunder and lightning
Is really quite frightening.

When you wake in the morning
And you sit up yawning,
And see the sun gleam,
You think it probably was a dream.

Alistair Harrison (10)
Cookham Rise Primary School

THE WILD, WILD JUNGLE

There the jungle stood before me,
Palm trees everywhere.
Bits of leaves and rockery,
It looked scary there.

I knew I wanted to go in,
So I took a chance.
I took a very deep breath,
And stepped into the world of trance.

As I walked through the jungle,
I heard a very strange sound.
Almost like a lion growling,
My heart began to pound.

Then to my great horror,
A monkey's face appeared.
He was cute and cuddly,
But suddenly disappeared.

So on I went through the jungle,
When I heard some thumping.
It was a herd of elephants,
All crying, laughing, bumping.

I ran and ran until I came,
Out of the other side.
I looked around for a minute or so,
I'm home again I cried!

Georgina Rickard (10)
Cookham Rise Primary School

CARIBBEAN

The Caribbean is very hot,
The sand white,
The sea, turquoise blue,
Palm trees swaying in the warm breeze,
The sun beaming down with its powerful rays.

Everyone having a fun time on the beach,
Dolphins making ripples on the ocean,
Children splashing at the waves,
Ships sailing away,
Tropical fish swimming in the sea.

People sunbathing under umbrellas,
Mums and dads blowing up rubber rings,
People snorkelling on the face of the sea.

Rachael Blair (9)
Cookham Rise Primary School

SPIDER!

Long, scuttly legs,
Running down the pipes,
Running down the pipes,
Big, black legs,
Climbing as they climb,
Climbing as they climb,
Big, hairy bodies,
In the centre of the legs,
In the centre of the legs.

Waiting in its web,
Waiting for its prey,
Its favourite sport,
Eating all the flies,
Splat!

Gina Chaplin (10)
Cookham Rise Primary School

THE WISHING CHAIR

I'd love to have a wishing chair,
I'd fly in it every day,
With candyfloss and a big funfair,
I want one right away
Just today!

Sophie Manzano (9)
Cookham Rise Primary School

EVERY DAY

Every day a blossom blooms,
Every day an aeroplane zooms,
Every day a field is watered,
Every day clocks have quarters,
Every day a baby is born,
Every day there is a storm,
Every day a flower is planted,
Every day there's something haunted,
Every day there's a cup of tea,
God bless everyone and me.

Laura Wyatt (8)
Cookham Rise Primary School

FOOTBALL

Football stadiums have brilliant atmospheres,
When you get there it's always packed,
As the manager and subs sit in the dug-out,
The manager must be sure, that he doesn't get sacked.

Passing all over the park,
As they try to score a goal,
But meanwhile having to defend,
When you score, everyone would like to see a forward roll.

Fans bellowing out,
And giving the players and managers stick,
Even when they score a goal,
The players must feel sick.

European teams get loads of money,
Teams challenging to stay up get no money,
It is really unfair,
The big clubs may find it funny.

Rory Millar (10)
Cookham Rise Primary School

School Days

We walked to school
Marc and me
A good three miles or more
Across the field
Through the lane
Right to the school house door.

Lee Flood (9)
Cookham Rise Primary School

A DAY IN YEAR 5

My bag is ready, I'm on my way
For yet another year 5 day
In the class I sit at my desk
Hoping we do not have a test
Then at lunchtime I go outside
I run around with my eyes open wide
Then I'm back in class with all the chatter
Oh I suppose it does not matter
Then it's time at last, to go home for my tea
I wonder if everyone likes year 5 like me.

Rebecca Hearn (10)
Cookham Rise Primary School

PIZZA

Tomato
Red tomato
Squashy red tomato
Yummy squashy red tomato
On my delicious pizza

Cheese
Yummy cheese
Smelly yummy cheese
Melted smelly yummy cheese
On my delicious pizza

Olive
Oily olive
Tasty oily olive
Big tasty oily olive
On my delicious pizza

Bread
Yummy bread
Tasty yummy bread
Delicious tasty yummy bread
On my delicious pizza

Veronica Settinieri (10)
Cookham Rise Primary School

SCHOOL

Horns toot
Lights flash
Everybody must dash
Hurry, hurry
Scurry, scurry
On my way to school

Crowded classrooms
Packed halls
People trying to act cool
Hurry, hurry
Scurry, scurry
First day back at school

Feet up
Box of chocs
CD on, door locked
Peace at last
Peace at last
Now I'm home from school

Helena Jones (10)
Cookham Rise Primary School

PETS

Puppy
Black puppy
Howling black puppy
Cute howling black puppy
Rolling in the mud
Puppy

                    Kitten
                    White kitten
                    Soft white kitten
                    Miaowing soft white kitten
                    Playing with some wool
                    Kitten

Anne-Marie Leonard (10)
Cookham Rise Primary School

THE BIG SPLASH

Gun sounds, off we race
Got to get a quicker pace
These are things I think you see
As my splashes say to me
Win, win, win.

My arms speed over my head
I will not be relegated
I will win without a doubt
My legs kicking seem to shout
Win, win, win.

Across the pool, we all dash
Faster, faster quick as a flash
As my hand touches the wall
My heart pounding seems to call
Won, won, won.

Rachael Taylor (10)
Cookham Rise Primary School

ELEPHANTS

Elephant
Daddy elephant
Gigantic daddy elephant
Frightening gigantic daddy elephant
Trudging through the green, green, green grass
Elephant

Elephant
Mummy elephant
Big mummy elephant
Scary big mummy elephant
Strolling through the green, green, grass
Elephant

Elephant
Baby elephant
Microscopic baby elephant
Playful microscopic baby elephant
Trotting through the green grass
Elephant.

Lisa Marie Carpenter (11)
Cookham Rise Primary School

BEWARE, BEWARE
(Based on the book, 'Beware, Beware' written by Susan Hill)

Bedroom's cosy
Curtains drawn,
Light's dim, candle burning,
But what's out there? Out there! Out there!

Night-time falls
Moon aglow.
Stars twinkle, winds blow.
But what's out there? Out there! Out there!
Who knows; shall I go?
Beware! Beware!

Slip on coat. Wrap round scarf.
Put on hat, lift the latch.
What's out here? Out here! Out here!
Beware! Beware!

Out here lies a wood
Deep, dark wood.
Leaves crunch. Owls hoot.
Branches like fingers. Full moon glows.
'I'm scared, I'm scared!'
Beware! Beware!

'Where are you?'
'I'm here. I'm here!'
Safe now, everything's fine.

Bedroom's cosy.
Curtains drawn. Lights dimmed, candle burning.
But what's out there?
I know. I know.

Elisa Girle (11)
Cookham Rise Primary School

NIGHT-TIME

Slowly up the creaking stairs
Clinging on to her teddy bears
Stripping off her shoes and socks
Putting skirt with all her frocks
Night-time, night-time, night-time

Slipping into her purple nightdress
Snuggling up with her teddy bear Tess
Closing her eyes to go to sleep
With Mum looking around to have a peep
Night-time, night-time, night-time.

Emma Sprules (11)
Cookham Rise Primary School

HOOVER

Big Hoover
Big roaring Hoover
Big roaring blowy Hoover

Little Hoover
Little roaring Hoover
Little roaring blowy Hoover

Massive Hoover
Massive roaring Hoover
Massive roaring blowy Hoover.

Joseph Clarke (11)
Cookham Rise Primary School

WAR

War is a killer
Lots of people die
The killing is a thriller
People can't stand to say goodbye
To poor people who have to go to war
War, war, war.

People lose legs
People get shot
People lose heads
When the battle is too hot
They all cry 'No more war!'
War, war, war.

Tom Crawforth (11)
Cookham Rise Primary School

FOOTBALL

Football boots covered in mud
No longer able to see a stud.
Hard tackles make players fall
As they lunge towards the ball.
Final whistle, final score
Once again, it's a draw!

Back in the changing room the
Manager roars
As players get kicked out the
Double doors.
Players threaten for a pay rise
Once again, the manager sighs.

Luke Matthews (10)
Cookham Rise Primary School

THE SIMPSON FAMILY

Homer,
Large Homer
Dumb, large Homer.
Bald, dumb, large Homer
Scoffing dinner like a lion
Homer.

Marge
Long-haired Marge
Smiling, long-haired Marge
Looking, smiling, long-haired Marge
Cleaning, cooking, washing for the family
Marge.

Bart
Cheeky Bart
Funny, cheeky Bart
Annoying, funny, cheeky Bart
Always getting told off
Bart

Lisa
Smart Lisa,
Nice smart Lisa
Good, nice, smart Lisa
Always getting 'A' in every test
Lisa

Maggie
Small Maggie
Smelly, small Maggie
Cute, smelly, small Maggie
Always sucking her dummy
Maggie.

Arunveer Singh Brar (11)
Cookham Rise Primary School

FERRETS

Ferrets
Baby ferrets
Slinky baby ferrets
Inquisitive slinky baby ferrets
Sleeping in the hay

Adult ferrets
Strong adult ferrets
Long strong adult ferrets
Hunting down their prey
Ferrets

Family of ferrets
Large family of ferrets
Cosy large family of ferrets
Loveable cosy large family of ferrets
Snuggling down together
Ferrets.

Victoria Tompkins (11)
Cookham Rise Primary School

RULES

Clean your teeth
Brush your hair
Don't leave stuff all over the stair.
'Hey! Don't you put that there!'
Rules, rules, here and there
Rules, rules are everywhere.

Clean your room
Do the washing-up
Hoover the sitting room
Chop, chop, chop!
'Open the window it's really hot.'
Rules, rules are here and there
Rules, rules are everywhere.

Rules, rules
Silly and dumb
But what would we do
Without them?

Naomi Lebens (11)
Cookham Rise Primary School

TRAVEL

Car
Fast car
Flashy fast car
Red flashy fast car
Speeding down the motorway
Car

Plane
Noisy plane
Huge noisy plane
White huge noisy plane
Gliding through the skies
Plane

Train
Speeding train
Smelly speeding train
Green smelly speeding train
Charging down the line
Train.

Andrew Withers (11)
Cookham Rise Primary School

WINTER

As the light-blue sky turned bleak and grey
Small mice were hibernating in the hay
The frosty air
And trees so bare
Were signs that winter was coming

There were children sledging, trying not to fall
And children building snowmen tall
The snow falling down
Down, down, down
Was a sign that winter was here.

The snow all gone
The sun half shone
Buds breaking through
As the blackbirds flew
These were all signs that winter was over.

Rebecca Ponter (11)
Cookham Rise Primary School

DOG CYCLE

Puppy
Newborn puppy
Cuddly newborn puppy
Playful cuddly newborn puppy
Napping in his basket
Puppy

Dog
Yapping dog
Mature yapping dog
Calm mature yapping dog
Walking by my side
Dog

Old dog
Aggressive old dog
Tired aggressive old dog
Sleeping on my bed
Old dog.

Laura Mack (11)
Cookham Rise Primary School

MOON LAND, MOON LAND

Moon land, moon land,
We're going to land.
Moon land, moon land,
We'll be first on the moon.
Moon land, moon land,
Look, the moon's getting closer!
Moon land, moon land,
Bang! We've landed.
Moon land, moon land,
Let's get some moon rock.
Moon land, moon land,
We're the first on the moon.
Moon land, moon land,
Put the flag in.
Moon land, moon land,
Back to Earth we go!

Joshua Gaeta (10)
Courthouse Junior School

DECEPTIVE TIME TRAVEL

Time travel is a deceptive thing,
Though I think it's fun.
Sometimes you can change your life,
But one mistake and you could die.

Don't worry
If you grow up mean.

Go back and change your evil ways,
I wish I could go back and change my mind about a toy.
But that's impossible
As everybody knows.
Time travel is impossible
Even I know.
There are some films about time travel,
I know because I've got some.
I suppose no one will ever know,
Why life was made so long ago.

Craig Lovell (10)
Courthouse Junior School

SKATE COASTER

I got this new skateboard yesterday,
This guy gave it to me.
Didn't have to pay,
The grip is first class.
It could even grip glass,
And don't mention the design.
Oh that's just fine.
So as you know I have to have a go.

Skate coaster, skate coaster
Wow!
Skate coaster, skate coaster
Back flip.
Skate coaster, skate coaster
900 I'm the king.
Skate coaster, skate coaster
Name it, I'll do it.
Skate coaster, skate coaster
This is unreal man!
Skate coaster, Paul come in
Noooo!

Paul Roberts (11)
Courthouse Junior School

FLOATING

Stars and planets all around,
How I wish to be back on the ground,
Floating in space all alone,
Discovering the amazing unknown.

Moving on, past Mars,
I prefer cars, to
Floating in space, all alone,
Discovering the amazing unknown.

Here comes the sun,
'Oh no! I'm done.'
Floating in space all alone,
Discovering the amazing unknown.

But it was kind of fun,
Apart from the sun,
Floating in space, all alone,
Discovering the amazing unknown.

Sam Greenland (10)
Courthouse Junior School

POETIC VOYAGES

Her ticket she could not find
She wanted to catch a bus to Hyde,
Reached in her coat pocket
What had she found?
She was being sucked into the never-ending ground,
Twisting and twirling down and down
Her feet didn't even reach the ground.

She found herself in space
Oh what a wonderful place,
Flying past constellations
Looking at space stations,
Dodging planets
Dodging stars
Had always thought Milky Ways were chocolate bars,
Then
Sucked in by a big black hole
Oh no! Where would she go?

She found herself at the bow of a ship
Hair soaking wet
Drip, drip, drip,
Storm brewed up
What bad luck,
Then came a wave nine metres high
Swallowed her up like an apple pie.

She found herself sinking in sand
Then on the floor with the bus ticket in her hand.

Jennifer Pollitt (10)
Courthouse Junior School

FAIR COASTER!

Calmly I gazed up at him,
Red shiny coat with polka-dot skin.
He was laughing hysterically at me.

It seemed like a statue,
(To the untrained eye!)
Just sitting there on his lines.
He made a slight move, and off he went!
Tearing down the drop.

Soon it was my turn,
To sit in his seats,
And cling on to his bar.

Then I waited for him to go
Tearing down the drop.
Then I would scream with my heart in my mouth,
And no noise would come,
that is until I'm off my bum, then call to my mum:
'I'm not going on that roller coaster again!'

Robert Leigh (11)
Courthouse Junior School

VIKING'S VOYAGE

Oars splashing,
Rain dancing,
Longboat glistens in the night
Sea bright
Sky getting light
Then the Vikings get a fright:
Huge serpent,
Dangerous serpent
Men shiver at the sight
Serpent thrashing
Longboat crashing.
Serpent wrapping round boat, tight.
People wailing
Serpent flailing
Then, silence in the night.

Douglas Gibbs (10)
Courthouse Junior School

SPACE

'Three, two, one, *blast-off!*
Away we go, going through space,
There goes the moon.'

'Away we go, going through space,
We're getting close to Pluto,
There goes Jupiter, that spot really does exist.'

'Away we go, going through space,
Still we're getting closer,
Uranus, Neptune - here it comes Pluto!'

Isn't this the end?

'Where are we?'
'Watch out! *No!*'

'There goes Pluto, back to Neptune,
Uranus, through Jupiter
There goes the moon, we're home.'

Alexander Davenport (11)
Courthouse Junior School

THE JOURNEY OF WRITING A POEM

Here I am, sitting in this room,
Above my head the teachers loom,
While I make up a poem to write,
I cannot think, my head is light.

I just sit here wasting time,
Trying to get the words to rhyme,
My mind is wandering again,
My pen is full, my page is plain.

What should I do, funny or sad?
After this lesson I will be glad.
My legs are jelly, my throat is tight,
This time I'll try with all my might.

'Put your pens down it is the end,'
I'm going to drive her around the bend.
'Twas just another day to me
But now it's over, time to flee!

Daniel Lambeth (11)
Courthouse Junior School

I'M FLYING

I'm flying, flying through the night
There's not a person in my sight,
All I see, way down below
Are lights merging, in a glow.

I feel the cruel wind touch my face
As I fly through the night to a secret place,
The flight takes me higher, then higher still,
As I gaze vaguely at my lost window sill.

I'm flying over London, flying over Hull
All I see as I cross the sea is a lost seagull.
I look down and my gaze goes too
The lost seagull and a ship that's blue.

As I go higher, climbing up
I see a cloud in the shape of a football cup.
Suddenly I burst through the cloud,
The cold makes me want to scream out loud.

But as I stare at the wondrous sight
The clouds seem to split with rays of sunlight.
All I could see were clouds and then,
The morning came, and I flew back again.

Stephen Jell (11)
Courthouse Junior School

A VOYAGE TO MY IMAGINATION

I am sitting in the classroom,
Lessons are such a bore.
I wish I was on the boat,
Sailing from the shore.

Sailing to the Caribbean,
Can't wait to get to shore.
Whenever I do, whenever I can,
I'm just gonna have *fun!*

I don't care where I sail,
As long as it's far away from school.
'This is lovely,' I said to the man.
'How much do I need to pay?'

Forgetting all my work,
I am still on my cruise.
What shall I do?
I don't have a clue.

'What do you think you are doing Sarah?' said Miss Williams.
'Pardon! Oh sorry Miss, I'm just on a holiday.'

Getting back on with my work
Finishing it off.
Will I ever get back
On my cruise from the shore?

Sarah Martindale (10)
Courthouse Junior School

EINSTEIN'S IDEA

Along the small creepy valleys
And under the dark quiet bridges,
Down streams and tiny pipes
Of red glossy blood;

Down the brain,
Past the eyes,
Who 'nose'
Where I am?

Maybe it was the nose
Or probably the ears,
And then the end
I was free;

I was out
I came out of one brain
And ended up in others.
I, Mr Fantastic Idea, was
Free!

Charisma Ghorpade (11)
Courthouse Junior School

A NATURE WALK WITH YEAR SIX
(AN UNEXPECTED VOYAGE)

As we all sat in silence, waiting for the day to begin
Miss Williams was looking at something,
And her face bore a small grin.

'Right!' she said in a voice that made the class sit up.
'We're going on a nature walk!'
And she slammed her book shut.

'What a bore!' groaned Ross Mulkern,
His shoe was squashing a snail,
His face was rather stern.

As we trudged on down the footpath the voice of Mr Brooks
Whispered 'Quiet everybody!
I thought I heard some rooks!'

Then we were put in groups to explore the deep dark woods,
I was grouped with Hannah, Sam and Ross,
Poor old Sam was made the boss!

Suddenly the Earth gave way; we were all surprised,
Down a hole and what we saw
Were monsters with googly eyes!

When we arrived at the bottom, we all landed with a thud!
We saw the king of the worm-like creatures,
And they weren't all covered in mud!

The king told us that they were woggies, he showed us the burrow,
The woggies were all hard at work,
Like there was no tomorrow!

The king said that it was time to go, he said bye to me and you
We arrived back safely on the ground,
But was it a dream or was it really true?

Laura Millyard (10)
Courthouse Junior School

DID IT HAPPEN?

Colours were flashing on my bedroom wall,
Could not move, did not know why
I started floating in the air
Before I knew it, I was whizzing everywhere.

I was sucked up through a colourful hole,
Colours flashing before my eyes,
Sounds thumping through my ears.

A ball of fire sizzling before my eyes,
I was going to crash,
Being burned to a frazzle
Is this a nightmare or a dream?

I pinched myself and there I was
Sitting on my bed, just as before.
It was not a nightmare,
It was not a dream
I think I had imagined it all!

Georgina Allen (10)
Courthouse Junior School

MY WORLD

My world, in my dreams, only visited by me.
My travel in my dreams to the seven continents of the world.

My journey starts at Antarctica going through to the Asian continent.

China, Japan, catch me if you can. I'm whizzing through space
in my dreams far away,
Turkey, Romania, Iraq, Arabia, I'm in a place where
day is night and night is day.

I'm travelling through China and into the middle, passing lots
of walls and trees.
It's like trying to solve a never-ending riddle, as grass and flowers
dance in the breeze.
But wait! What's this? It's the humungous 'Great Wall'.
Its spiral staircase made of stone and all,
It's like a long snake, grey and tall, people say it will never cease.

Now I'm tired of this Asia, and I'll fly over Australasia
to the American continents.

Now my mind takes us to the land of North America, the place where
thousands of things just happen to be,
Piling around the different places, that I can imagine and that I can see.
There's the White House, ever so white, reflecting the water,
reflecting the light.
But ever so recently, President decisions between Gore and Bush,
it was a competition.
Sadly Gore went on fire and wrestled with the flames,
Bush just sat and played cheering games.
I think that's enough for now, except that I voted for Gore, but now
who cares, because that's no more.

I think I'll pass South America and travel to North Africa instead.

Let's move east to the country of Egypt, the place where there're
pyramids everywhere.
The place where myths and rumours are started, the place where
there's a pharaoh's lair. Tutankhamen!
The pharaoh, the king, the greatest man.
The king who told his slaves to work across in his almighty land,
Now this is known because of hieroglyphics, the symbols
on walls that were once bare,
These symbols are almost everywhere, including Tutankhamen's lair.

I've got an urge to go to Europe, my final destination.

Rome, a historic land with places made of pearls and places so grand.
The Coliseeum, a building where battles of life and death took place.
Where Gladiators swung their axes and flung their swords and mace,
I think that's enough violence for a long time and now let's go to
Augustus' house, if we're allowed.
And yes! The Palatine Hall, it's a place where tourists will always call.

My dreams end with me having gone around the world.
I will not share this with anyone, for it is my world.

Gurpreet Bharya (10)
Courthouse Junior School

HIGHER, HIGHER, HIGHER

Whenever the teachers start to drone
I drift away in a world of my own.
Higher and higher up in the sky:
Dull division I leave behind.

Leaving pupils with hanging heads
Slipping through the skylight everyone else looks dead.
Fun is soaring, way up high
See that jumbo jetting by?

A shimmering shining ball of fire,
Just think what would happen if I went higher.
The only thing that's stopping me is
A clean cotton cloud with a fluffy white feel.

Dring, dring, dring!
I'm back to the drool
The bell has rung and it's the end of school.
Homework tonight and then it's bed
But when tomorrow comes I can fly again.

Harriet Pridmore (10)
Courthouse Junior School

MURDEROUS STAIRS

Tom sat playing with his toys,
His mother called the dreaded words 'Bedtime, now be a good boy.'
He knew this would mean he would have to climb the dreaded stairs,
He had fought the dragon, wrestled the lion, teased the alligator and
tied the snake in a knot, without a care.
While he sat clearing his toys he wondered what would await him
at the top.
Slowly, slowly Tom reached the stairs, he gasped with the shock!
Awaiting him, stood talking blocks that pinched you,
White thin ghosts floating and watching you too.
Dolls pulling off their heads and swapping with each other,
Walking towards him and calling 'Mamma, mamma!'
He took on the challenge and started climbing,
First were white ghosts watching, Tom walked on trying to
stop minding.
Tom knew the only way to win the battle was to put on shoes and stamp
on the sheets,
He left the now muddy dead sheets on the stairs and carried on up
with bare feet.
Next were the blocks, Tom swung his foot back and kicked as hard as
he could, the blocks went flying!
Although it hurt his foot and he couldn't help crying,
He looked up and saw the dolls; they were all asking him to swap heads
He picked up the dolls and threw them to the bottom where their arms
broke and so did their legs.
Tom had won the battle, he called his trusty horse, which was only a
Shetland pony, whose name was Rover!
They charged to his room and dived under the cover.

Annie Godfrey (11)
Courthouse Junior School

A SPACE EXPERIENCE

I'm going on a voyage,
Whilst sitting in this chair,
I'm going on a voyage
But I really don't know where.

Crashing into Jupiter,
Flying right past Mars,
Observing Earth from different angles,
Staring at the stars.

Travelling light years every minute,
Shooting through the air,
Whizzing at top speed now,
Charging without a care.

Turning round I see a comet,
I twist and turn as I begin to fall,
And land in my chair
After all.

Stephanie Rowan (10)
Courthouse Junior School

VOYAGE OF A TEN PENCE PIECE

I'm here
I'm lying,
No one to hear that I think I'm dying.

Until
A boy picks me up,
No longer steady and still,
I'm in luck.

He spends me
On a few penny sweets,
And that's where I'll be
In the counter, back to the old me.

I'm set free
Thanks to a girl who made me change,
But now I have the world to see
This is because I fell out of the pocket with all the bits and bobs.

Rolling and tumbling into the drains
In the streets where they're found.
Turning and tumbling and falling down,
And that's where I am now found.

Nathacia-Mary Sikkel (10)
Courthouse Junior School

THE BIRD OF LIFE

Splashes of colour across the enchanted bird,
Phoenix-like tail feathers, blue,
It swoops down and carries me upwards.
Soft wings, which I cling on to
Swoop over countries far and near.

The bird flies on as a speck in the sky,
Brushing against the treetops high;
I can see for many miles in this bird-like style,
Deserted land is all I can find,
Swoop over countries low and high.

The beautiful bird flies low,
I look around the new land found.
People around me smile,
They bow to me like we've always been friends;
What a joyful time! I hope it never ends.
Swoop over countries, high and low.

The weather is freezing,
Through a blizzard we fly,
We're heading north, the courageous bird struggles on forth.
On the ground I see a lonely child playing with a seal,
How bad I feel.
Swoop over countries, happy and sad.

Far from where we started, we finally land,
In a country dotted with bags of sand.
Shots ring out, vibrations hum,
I feel so strange, so hurt, something is wrong,
I turn to go, I want to run but the bird of life has gone.

Catherine Sayer (10)
Courthouse Junior School

THE LIGHT OF THE WORLD

A bird lands beside me
And spreads out its wings,
All colours are bright, glistening in the light,
I squint in the brightness,
The bird hovers over me and disappears!

The room fills with whiteness, all fluffy and soft,
Suddenly a door appears,
I walk up to it and *flash!*
I think what? That's the bird again.

The bird swoops down beside me as I am falling
And lifts its head.
It swoops again, catches me this time!
Its golden wings, feather out wider,
It lands for a short time.
I feel great fright as the bird takes flight!

The bird says 'Hi, I'm the Firebird!'
I ask 'Bird of all light?'
'Yes'
I'm astonished and feel weird.

He takes me to a room,
I'm in the future, in my house.
Everything's dark and dull
And suddenly bright!
I go to stroke the bird's feathers,
But fall to a fluffy room,
My bedroom!

Gemma Bartholomew (10)
Courthouse Junior School

HOT SCALDING DESERT

Hot scalding desert
I'm struggling with the heat,
And with the ground getting hotter
I'm starting to burn my feet.

Hot scalding desert
What am I going to do?
With sand as hot as fire
I haven't got a clue.

Hot scalding desert
With sand that's miles long,
And as I run to get to the end
The wind starts singing a song.

Hot scalding desert
With camels rushing by
And being away from home so long
I sit down and start to cry.

Linda Parker (11)
Courthouse Junior School

WHEEEE!

Small, small and even smaller as I get miniaturised,
I call for help but nobody hears me,
Suddenly I begin to fall, but then something catches me,
It's a flying washing basket, yippee!

Oops I just remembered it's my mum, she is doing the
                                        dirty washing,
Through into the utility room,
She then begins to put the powder in,
Slowly she opens the door and pushes me and the clothes in.

The dial then begins to turn,
It's time for me to say goodbye,
Suddenly, because I'm so small, I fall down a hole,
Deeper and deeper into the machine I tumble.

Ross Pepper (11)
Courthouse Junior School

A STORMY SAIL

I can feel my heavy eyes shutting, I force to keep them open,
Suddenly I'm on a boat, sailing on the ocean,
Oh no! A storm is raging to my left, not far off,
A wave just splashed on my head,
Now tiny waves are hitting me, ouch!
Another wave soaks my head, a cold one,
A siren is singing to me, although I cannot see her,
Crack! Aaah the mast has broken,
The water's closing in around my feet,
Now I feel dry, how can that be, it must be the soil,
Is this really what it's like to die?

Voices are ringing in my ears,
My eyes focus, I sit up,
My face is covered in dinner, not much on my plate,
Suddenly from my hair falls a drip, that wasn't there before,
Pain surges through my body, my sister's hands are red,
A tea towel is spread over me,
Mum is shouting at my sister,
Dad is humming his new tune,
What could've happened in such a very short time?

Leila Gilhooly (10)
Courthouse Junior School

INSIDE OUT

A fish called Wolly, I was
Anything but adventurous because
A shark who happened to pass by
Took a liking to the glint in my eye.

So much he liked what he saw
A bite out of me he did gnaw,
The first bite it tasted so good,
One more bite? Yes he thought that he would.

So inside his mouth I was stuck,
And it looked like I'd run out of luck,
Down his throat I was moving (it was really quite soothing)
While I slithered and wriggled and bucked.

With a splash I was into his tum,
His stomach was full of green gum,
With the crabs, shrimps and eels he'd eaten some seals,
Along with a portion of rum!

As I passed through his upper intestines,
The colours were really quite interesting.
All the blues, greens and reds, mixed up with fish heads
Was really not what you'd get dressed in!

I finally arrived at the end,
As I went round the last of the bends,
My head popped out and with a final shout
I shot out like a bullet, Amen.

Hannah Evans (10)
Courthouse Junior School

A NIGHT IN THE STARLIGHT

On a page of this book, it surely amazes,
The magic that's done with a handful of phrases.
So when I read this book I start off quite early,
For when I turn the leaves, I am off on a journey . . .

Shooting stars, comets and planets galore,
As out into space I can feel myself soar!
Twisting and racing - faster than fast,
Away from the Earth and out into the dark.

I am sailing past Jupiter, Saturn and Mars,
I see a black hole sucking in all the stars.
I then turn my face to look at the sun,
A million gasses collected in one.

As to the edge of the galaxy I go,
A large shining star puts on a show,
First it explodes, then shrivels and dies,
It did not effect me - that is a surprise.

I see signs of the Zodiac standing together,
Gemini, Cancer - they'll be there forever.
I wish not to leave - but it's time for lights out,
I want to know what the next page is about,
If I wait till tomorrow, I soon will find out.

Emmy Alghabra (11)
Courthouse Junior School

THROUGH THE MIRROR

I went through the mirror
In my mum's room,
And landed on a bed made of food,
There were crisps, cakes and sweets galore,
And after all that my tummy was sore.
I went to the bathroom (because I felt sick),
But all I found was a gigantic lollipop stick,
I walked round the bathroom to check it out,
I crawled to the bathtub and guess what I found,
50,500 fun-size Time Outs.
I thought I'd been gone for hours,
I went through the mirror to eat my dinner,
But when I arrived back it was still twenty past two,
Still no one knows where I went that day,
So I say enjoy the happy days while they stay.

Rachel Mercy (10)
Courthouse Junior School

IMAGINATION

Drifting through water,
Flying through the air,
Running across land,
Swirling through space.
Time passes . . .
In the real world my mother calls,
My book lies motionless on my desk.
Traffic goes by outside,
I neither see nor hear.
Memories of time flash by,
My mind is dragged away by magic.
Somersaulting through unseen life.
Falling, falling onto a soft bed of feathers,
Echo, echo, echo,
A million miles away in another universe my mind spins,
Dragged through shivering stardust.
On a voyage in my imagination,
Blinded by light,
I am not awoken,
My glazed eyes staring, staring,
Pulled through past, present, future,
On, on into Storyland my mind sleeps on.
My physically awake body keeps sitting, staring.
I cartwheel away from life,
Life . . . Life is a virtue.

Eleanor Fricker (10)
Courthouse Junior School

BOUNCY BABY

As I gaze at my little brother
His wistful blue eyes staring into nothingness . . .
What in the world do babies think?
What in the world indeed!

I reckon, babies must have journeys every day
In the wild depths of their imaginations,
Climbing on pillow mountains
And putting a flag at the top.
Babies must have journeys every day.

Shapes ever forming in their small minds,
Minds so small and yet so humungous,
Trekking through jungles dark and fiery,
And wrestling a tiger to the floor,
Shapes ever forming in their small minds.

Babies must have journeys every day,
Crawling through Sweetland grabbing chocolate lollies,
Using them to vault over treacle lakes
And catching the 'wheels go round' bus home,
Babies must have journeys every day.

You never can tell what a baby is thinking,
If you could you'd be totally amazed
At all the wonders you would find,
But you never can tell what a baby is thinking.

Sophie Lyons (10)
Courthouse Junior School

I'M GOING TO THE FUTURE

I'm going to the future,
Then whizzing back again.
One minute I'm a hundred,
The next minute I'm ten.

I go back to the dinosaurs,
See an iguanodon,
This journey is fantastic,
And it's only just begun!

I watch a pterodactyl,
It dives then starts to soar,
Lays its caught fish on a rock
Then eats the catch raw.

Fast-forward to the future
With hi-tech aliens green and slimy,
They stare at me, then throw some slime,
I thought 'yuk!' Then 'blimey!'

Rush back to the present,
Not future, nor the past,
My first time experience
Which might not be my last!

Ben Stuart (9)
Courthouse Junior School

THE RADIO WHIRLS

I was listening to the radio,
I started to think about my problems.
The music faded in my ears,
I was in darkness spinning rapidly, slowly then fast,
Squeaking and squealing filled my ears,
Patterns and shapes filled my eyes,
People's faces and comments from the previous day
                                    blurred my mind.
Mad laughing made me sweat, doomed and scared
I looked around but it was just blackness.
Then the blackness faded too,
Scenes popped out of my head as fast as they came in
As if on a television with someone flicking the channels,
It settled with one scene in the future.
My name was engraved on a tombstone,
In a graveyard my family were mourning my death
While a grave digger dressed in black walked to my family
And shoved them laughing, they landed thud on my coffin.
I woke with my heart beating as heavily as the next track on the radio.

Elli Thatcher Jones (10)
Courthouse Junior School

BOAT TRIP

'We're going on a boat trip,'
Mum said one day.
'To where?' I asked back.
'Caribbean' she answered.
I was so excited as we were leaving today.
We're going on a boat trip,
My brother sang out
As we skipped along the seashore to our boat.
'I'm choosing which bunk I'm going on first,'
I shouted out as we got in the cabin.
I chose the very top bunk,
But of course my brother had to sleep next to me.
We started when the horn went off,
Which was very soon, 'barp' . . .
We were off!
I had never felt as excited as this in my life.
As soon as we set off I felt seasick.
It was time to go to sleep for my brother and I.
My brother snores,
So I couldn't get to sleep half the night.
Next morning Mum bustled me up,
She said it was half an hour until we got off the boat.
I got up quickly and brushed my teeth ready to go.
'Wow!' I screamed as we reached the shore,
It was a sandy beach, we walked to our hotel.

Holly Bennett (10)
Courthouse Junior School

MERMAID AND ME

In the water, in the sea,
I found a mermaid swimming to me!
She had a dolphin, its name was Bubble,
She was sweet and she never caused trouble.
We looked for treasure and we looked for shells,
We found something, two golden bells.
I asked her name, she said 'It's Loretta,'
Then we played a game it got better and better.
She asked me if I'd like to come for tea,
I said, 'What are we having?'
She said, 'Seaweed.'
Afterwards we went to bed,
This has been a brill day I thought in my head.
When I woke I found a starfish,
Then Loretta woke and served me a dish.
It was time for me to go,
So we swam to the surface of the sea,
Then she said that she would miss me.

Katie Alston (9)
Courthouse Junior School

ALIEN WORLD

In my mind I see a world,
A long, long time from now.
The sea is green,
The land is silver,
Shiny all around.

Everything is blinding,
I see suns everywhere
And on the ground,
What's going on?
There are little aliens
Unlike you and me.

The aliens are as small as cats,
They're orange and they're cute,
They wear black suits
And boots as well,
And they're very friendly *chaps.*

Then a hovering thing comes,
Yellow and not that big.
And on it, there are thirteen
Of these little alien things.

Some get off and more get on,
All bobbing up and down.
And I wonder if their transport
Is ever as late as mine!

Erif Newman (9)
Courthouse Junior School

SPELLBOUND

I'm sitting on my bed, reading a book
And just about to open the front page,
Feeling a sensational tingly feeling,
Oh, I'm being sucked in my book!

Looking around with a puzzled face,
Finding myself on a train,
Carrying new, jet-black robes,
Wondering, is this a dream?

Helping myself to some chocolate frogs,
Sitting right next to a boy,
Jet-black hair, a lightning scar,
Not knowing where we were going.

A dark, eerie castle appeared,
Gloomy trees scattered here and there,
Stumbling into a huge hall,
Walking into a silvery school.

I stayed in the book for hours and hours,
Dumfounded by everything,
Helping defeat an evil wizard,
Oh, what a time I am having.

Creeping through my door at night,
Looking for a way out of the book,
A huge, roaring gust of winding wind
Has lifted me out of the book!

Bryony Holt (9)
Courthouse Junior School

OFF TO WALES

We're off to Wales, we're off to Wales,
Through the tunnel and dodge the rails.
Over the bridge jiggidy jig,
Over the mound, don't make a sound.
Round the corner, up the ramp,
Jump the rock through the stream,
Down the ramp, turn the corner,
Through the reef, see the coral,
Hear the fish blabbing away.
We're nearly there, we're nearly there,
Half a mile to go.
Across the meadow, squash the daisies,
On to the path,
We're there, we're there!
Now down to the beach,
Jump in the sea, gosh goosepimples it's so cold!
Oh what a day.

Georgina Fidler (9)
Courthouse Junior School

AN IMAGINARY VOYAGE

I was sitting in an armchair a long time ago,
Reading a voyage book about things in the past.
Here I read for hours, each line over again,
Thinking about if I was there,
At that place with the old ship in the book.
My imagination took off and I felt I was there.
Some people with hats all covered in flowers
Were rolling some rope into an old ship.
I saw an island far away on a distant shore,
Really I wondered if they were travelling there.
Still I stood rooted there,
One of the men turned round,
All the other men turned round too.
They all heaved me into their big brown ship.
They all smiled and talked to me,
Really I felt I was one of them,
A dog ran out of the cabin base
Chasing after a mouse,
He ran up to me and grabbed my skirt
But I didn't really care much.
Here I was on a ship, a lifetime journey
Over the deep blue sea.

Louise Rayfield (10)
Courthouse Junior School

Death Run!

In the dark of midnight
I awake inside my coffin.
As I get steady
I open my eyes and mind.
My journey begins through the graveyard,
Creeping as I walk.
Scampering around to find my way
To Heaven's gates.
As I pass grounds of graves,
Reading all the names.
Then I remembered
The weeping willow where I died,
How I hung myself.
Scampering and struggling to find my way,
At last I got there,
Pushed over the gates.
Now I'm in Heaven
Having too much fun,
But I will never forget my
Death run!

Kelly-Anne Chivers (10)
Courthouse Junior School

WHAT WILL IT BE LIKE IN THE FUTURE?

Travelling through time
    Into the future,
Wondering what it would
    Be like.

Finding things that might
    Be in the future,
Or things that are history
    Of the past.

Seeing what people
    Might do,
Maybe there will be robots,
    Who knows?

Perhaps we won't have
    To go to school,
Now that would be
    A *miracle!*

Finding things that
    Might happen,
Like earthquakes or
    Volcanoes erupting.

Wondering if there will
    Be a future,
Or maybe we'll be stuck
    In the past!

Cara Guest (10)
Courthouse Junior School

TRAVELLING IN THE PAST

Travelling in the past
Feels like you're travelling through the air,
Reds, blues, purples and yellows
All swirling and mixing together.

Bright green doors flashing with colour
Which you can open with your tiny little hands,
Inside the door is a date,
Like 1958.

Whichever year you want to go in
Just drift in and see what it's like,
If you don't like the year
Quickly run out!

Keep travelling and travelling in the past
Until you want to turn back,
So you turn around, open every door
Until you find the right year.

Go in the door and stay there forever,
But you will be carrying on the years before you
Like nothing has ever happened.

Linda Third (9)
Courthouse Junior School

FISH'S UNDERWATER JOURNEY

Bubbles streaming from my mouth,
I looked ahead and spied the coral reef.
Bright colours of the fish that swam whizzing past me,
Seaweed dancing in the water, all fresh and green with glee.
Looking behind, my mind went flash,
A great white shark was right by my tail.
Fins went wild, 'Time to swim.'
So I swam as fast as I could.
Fishes were a blur of colours,
Also scared right down to the bone.
At last I found a huge black rock
Standing by my side.
My tail swung so did my body.
Hidden by the huge black rock
My fins relaxed and fell back in relief.

Lucie Lapham (9)
Courthouse Junior School

In My Imagination

Travelling in my imagination is wonderful.
Bursting out of the room on strong silver wings.
Clouds are drifting across the sky without a care in the world.
Slowly the clouds get dark, changing from light blue to dark black.

Stars come out, twinkling with a dazzling white light.
Set out below me, like a beautiful detailed picture is the world.
Looking up I can see the man in the moon beckoning me.
So I fly up, say 'Hi,' and try some soft green cheese.

Starting to feel sleepy I relax on air, and go to sleep.
Later I wake up happy and refreshed.
Seeing the sea I fly far down, the cold, salty water sprays me.
Copying the seagulls I fly down skimming the waves.

Diving down into the cold, black water I retrieve a fish,
But seeing its look of pain I throw it back, where it
                          swims away happily.
Flying up to London, I hear Big Ben strike twelve so I fly off
And go home again.

Rachel Ashe (9)
Courthouse Junior School

ROCKY ROMANS

Back in time I have been,
Roman times I went to,
To see all the wonderful things they had.
They had many things we don't have now,
Like Emperors and togas.
They used numerals and talked in Latin,
And famous statues which are in pieces now,
I really liked it there.
It had a big empire in Italy, parts of Britain
And many, many more,
It was the best place ever.
There was many places to go
And they were all different every time.
Suddenly I went back to today's life
And how different it was.

Kristina Butler (9)
Courthouse Junior School

TIME TRAVEL

Travelling back in time, *it's great!*
Finding out all sorts of things, learning it's annoying
If you haven't listened to the teacher,
But this is great, time travelling,
Back to the beginning of time.
Where am I? With these people surrounding me,
It must be the Tudors because look there's Henry,
Big, fat Henry VIII.
Ah, where am I going? I'm travelling once again,
Where will I go, in my imagination?
Look there's William, William the Conqueror, what's he doing here?
Ah, run, he's chasing me, it must be the Norman Conquest.
I'm travelling, I'm travelling, they will wonder where I've gone!
I'm still wondering where I've gone?
Oh it must be the Romans, there is a Roman's big shield,
But no more time for poetry, we have to fight. 'Hiya Boff,'
Ha, ha I've killed you, oh so soon I was enjoying this.
Oh no it's the Romans' big goodbye, bye from me too.
Oh no it's the teacher, I must be back at school,
She'll tell me I've been daydreaming again,
But secretly I'll know I've been time travelling.

Sarah Wilson (9)
Courthouse Junior School

THROUGH THE SEASONS

Lily pads upon the pond,
  Daisies, roses and acorn trees.
Long, hot, boiling days,
  Paddling pools are put away.

The leaves are falling,
  Red, brown and crisp.
Crunch and crackle,
  Under my wellington boots.

The pond has frozen over,
  Snow is coming down.
Children are playing snowballs
  In the cold, freezing air.

Bluebells are appearing,
  So is blossom too.
Trees are almost fully grown,
  The sun is out for summer.

Harriet Burdett (9)
Courthouse Junior School

THE FOUR SEASONS

As I was walking to my friend's house
I saw a boy on his bike.
The wheels whizzed around and reminded
Me of the four seasons in a year.

First comes . . . Winter, it is snowy and fun,
    Make a snowman or,
    Throw snowballs at each other,
    Wrap up warm with a hat and scarf.

Then comes . . .Spring, the weather is getting hotter,
    Wear less warm clothes,
    Go to the park with a friend,
    While Mum and Dad book the holidays.

Next comes . . . Summer, the best season of the year,
    Summer holidays are soon,
    School is out,
    Time to have fun on *holiday.*

Last comes . . . Autumn, animals collect food,
    Ready for the long winter's hibernation,
    Leaves crunch underfoot,
    Orange, yellow, brown.

Now I'm outside my friend's house,
I tell her all about my imaginary voyage,
We played games and I got home in time for tea.

Bianca Heath (9)
Courthouse Junior School

TRAVEL SICKNESS

Departing from the port of Dover,
Stepping on to the ferry
I just can't wait until it's over
When I look into the deep, dark sea.

Trying to look as if it's great fun
Though turning green and feeling sick,
And even worse when the thought occurs to me,
Look what happened to the Titanic!

Getting nearer every day
I'm dreaming of the shore,
My mother said, 'We'll be there in a week.'
But I can't take it anymore.

This is it! I'm here!
No more tumbling waters or splashing waves,
A seat that won't move,
A bed that won't sway,
I just wish I didn't have to go home again!

Julia Walton (10)
Courthouse Junior School

MY TEDDY

I'd like to be a wrestler
And win every title there,
But even if I was a millionaire
I still would need my bear.

I'd like to be a racer
And race whenever I want,
But even if I won the race
I still would need my bear.

I'd like to be a DJ
And stay up later than you,
But even if I had my mates
I still would need my bear.

I'd like to be in a cartoon
And do the silly things they do,
But even if I made you laugh
I still would need my bear.

Imran Hussain (10)
Ellington Primary School

ONE ORANGE BIRD

One orange bird sitting in the nest.
Two triangle telephones phoning their friends.
Three oak trees standing in the dark.
Four flowers flying to the sun.
Five orange sausages sizzling in the pan.
Six fat snowmen sitting in the sun.
Seven fat snakes going to the river.
Eight big elephants walking in the water.
Nine thin snakes running in the park.
Ten fat men sitting in the armchair.

Rizwana Mahmood
Ellington Primary School

THE STORM

The storm is strong,
It blows the houses,
It makes thunder,
And blows the trees
And straw houses,
Sometimes it rains.
It rumbles and tumbles
All the time.
Some people don't
Like the storm,
Some people do.
I don't like the storm
But I like the rain.
People like water but
People do not like the storm.

Valerie Kondo (8)
Ellington Primary School

GRAN'S PETS

In Gran's parlour she kept
Ten fleas that hopped about,
Nine rats who ate the furniture,
Eight bats with round eyes,
Seven rabbits that chased each other,
Six lions that crashed into things,
Five hippos under the chair,
Four horses in the wardrobe,
Three sabre-toothed tigers that looked fierce,
Two dragons that flew around,
And one . . . *guess what!*

Michael Kirton (9)
Furze Platt Junior School

CATS' NIGHT

Cats at night, some black, some white,
Getting in a fight,
They scratch and bite,
That's what they do at night.

Sam Carter (8)
Furze Platt Junior School

AT ASNIERES

Not only the glistening blue of the river,
No.
Not only the yacht drifting,
No.
Not only the drop of rain that never came,
No.
Not only the bathers washing their faces,
No.
Not only the dog panting
Steadily.

Juliet Clark (8)
Furze Platt Junior School

AT ASNIERES I SAW . . .

At Asnieres I saw . . .
The turquoise river shimmering under the bridge,
A boy's clothes left to dry in the sun, warm and bright,
A distant factory, the smoke floating peacefully
Till a crack, a deckchair broke but people
Just looked around and didn't say a word.

Siân Osborn (8)
Furze Platt Junior School

ON HOLIDAY

A couple of children in the blue river,
A dog wagging its tail up and down.
A glistening sun reflecting off the blue river.
I could see a factory in the background,
Smoke flowing in the breeze,
Polluting the summer's air.
All was quiet until the dog barked.

Christopher Watts (9)
Furze Platt Junior School

GRANNY'S PETS

In my granny's bedroom, she kept
Ten elephants that stomped around the room,
Nine Siberian tigers that snarled and prowled,
Eight hedgehogs scuttling and sniffing,
Seven dragons breathing smoke,
Six red squirrels climbing up her dress,
Five monkeys screeching with laughter,
Four donkeys hiding in the cupboard,
Three rats creeping round,
Two frogs leaping up and down,
And one . . . *guess what!*

Isobelle Vernon-Smith (9)
Furze Platt Junior School

NOT ONLY THE . . .

Not only the faded green of the grass,
No.
Not only the water glistening and sparkling,
No.
Not only the smoke from the factories,
No.
Not only the bathers' clothes all crumpled,
No.
Not only the bather with cupped hands
Whistling.

Stuart Shepherd (9)
Furze Platt Junior School

NOT ONLY THE . . .

Not only the light of the boat moving,
No.
Not only the water flowing beside the bank,
No.
Not only the black smoke coming from the factory,
No.
Not only the people swimming in the water,
No.
Not only the dog laying on the floor too lazy to bark,
Licking himself.

Ryan Simmonds (8)
Furze Platt Junior School

WHAT ELSE?

Not only the faded green of the grass,
No.
Not only the water glistening like a diamond,
No.
Not only the yachts skimming across the water,
No.
Not only the trees swaying in the breeze,
No.
Not only the man's clothes lying on the bank.

Jessica Whitworth (9)
Furze Platt Junior School

BATHERS ON THE BANK

Not only the bright white of the sail,
No.
Not only the trees swaying in the breeze,
No.
Not only the drop of rain that never came,
No.
Not only the bathers' clothes which lay on the bank,
No.
Not only the dog lying on the grass.

James Cawthorpe (8)
Furze Platt Junior School

WHAT I SAW AT ASNIERES

At Asnieres I saw
The water glistening in the hot sun,
A punt sailing through the water like a slow snake,
The factory gently puffing out smoke in the distance,
A bather swimming in the turquoise, cool river,
The man's crumpled, boiling clothes,
Till a splash made by a swimmer,
But they still wanted complete silence,
The dog growled but the people couldn't speak,
Because it was so hot.

Nicola Courtier (8)
Furze Platt Junior School

AT ASNIERES

At Asnieres I saw
A dog panting quietly,
A blue river shining,
A factory in the distance chuffing out smoke,
Just then a loud splash came,
It was someone jumping in the water.

Rachel Christian (9)
Furze Platt Junior School

ASNIERES

Not only the breeze taking the factories' smoke who knows where
No,
Not only the river glimmering in the steaming hot sun
No,
Not only the men in the river happily swaying side to side
No,
Not only some men with their hats on to block the sun
No,
Not only the men's clothes in a heap on the bank
No,
Not only the dog's tongue and her steady panting.

Ryan Jones (9)
Furze Platt Junior School

MY ANIMAL POEM

Cats - leaping,
Birds - flying,
Fish - swimming,
Humans - walking,
Cats - purring,
Cats - striking,
Tigers - go for the kill,
Crabs - pinch,
Lions - camouflage,
Cheetahs - run fast,
Leopards - sleep.

Robert Ashburner (8)
Furze Platt Junior School

NOT ONLY THE...

Not only the deep blue sea of the water,
No.
Not only the bathers resting in the hot sun,
No.
Not only the hot sun like a furnace,
No.
Not only the light green of the swaying trees,
No.
Not only the dog's tongue hoping for water.

Malcolm Gledhill (9)
Furze Platt Junior School

THE CLASS

Today we are so busy,
I don't know what to do,
Where is little Lizzie?
'I don't know' said Sue.

'Why don't you go outside?'
'What shall we play?'
'You seek, I'll hide,'
That's what Sue would say!

Kirsty Arena (9)
Furze Platt Junior School

A HOT DAY

At Asnieres I saw
Water glimmering in the sun,
Calm as a sleeping lion,
A yacht shining and reflecting in the water,
A dozing man bathing in the red-hot sun,
A factory in the distance,
And some crumpled clothes all warm,
Then the hungry dog started barking.

Erik Williams (8)
Furze Platt Junior School

THE SUNNY DAY

At Asnieres I saw . . .
A turquoise river with traces of the sun,
Silence apart from the thirst-quenching dog,
His owner sunbathing by the water's edge,
The sun just going down behind the horizon,
Clothes crumpled in a heap,
One person dipping his toes in the cool flowing water,
A young boy sipping water from his cupped hands.

Amelia Hendry (9)
Furze Platt Junior School

NOT ONLY . . .

Not only the beautiful blue water,
No.
Not only the panting dog,
No.
Not only the factory's smoke,
No.
Not only the trees swaying in the breeze,
No.
Not only the pretty yachts,
No.

Tom Watts (8)
Furze Platt Junior School

BATHERS ON THE BANK

Not only the green grass swishing,
No.
Not only the brown trees swaying,
No.
Not only the black dog woofing,
No.
Not only the man's clothes hot and crispy,
No.
Not only the hot people breathing.

Hannah Heales (9)
Furze Platt Junior School

DOG IN THE HOUSE

I see a dog
Slyly and carefully running,
Eyes open, as wide as can be,
Nose sniffing hard,
Ears pricked up,
Tail wagging like mad,
Jumping as high as ever,
Calm now, the door has shut.

Fleur Hughes (9)
Furze Platt Junior School

THE BATHERS AT ASNIERES

Not only the boiling sun beating on the bathers,
No.
Not only the rainy day that never came,
No.
Not only the factory smoking in the distance,
No.
Not only the trees hanging still in the breeze,
No.
Not only the boats who had just enough wind to move.

Jake Leonard (8)
Furze Platt Junior School

MICE

They live in a box
And eat old socks.

They eat chocolate,
They eat a lot of it.

They nibble things they should not touch,
And no one likes them very much.

They scurry about the house all night,
They go to sleep when it's light.

Their enemy is the pussy cat
Who sleeps on the tartan mat.

Georgina Kirkwood (8)
Furze Platt Junior School

WAR

War is an oozy yellow,
It smells of mouldy cheese.
War tastes of filthy rubbish,
It sounds like nails on a chalkboard.
War feels like burning fire,
War lives in a sewer.

Daniel Love (9)
Furze Platt Junior School

HOPE

Hope is light pink and blue,
It smells like liquorice and lilies.
Hope tastes as sweet as sugar and spice
And all things nice.
It sounds like blue tits singing in the morning
And owls hooting in the evening.
Hope feels warm and tingly,
It lives up in the warm mountains
Where the flowers and rabbits live!

Lucy Higgon (10)
Furze Platt Junior School

HOPE

Hope's colours are pink, blue and white,
It smells like sweet innocent perfume.
Hope tastes like mouth-watering sweets,
It sounds like birds singing sweetly.
Hope feels very silky, like velvet,
It lives in a huge tree trunk, glittering in the sunlight.

Heidi Goldsmith (9)
Furze Platt Junior School

HOPE

Hope is violet,
It smells like springtime flowers,
It tastes like ice cream,
It sounds like high-pitched opera singers,
It feels like soft silk,
It lives in a golden place.

Nicola Skidmore (9)
Furze Platt Junior School

SNOWMAN

Glistening white,
Snow upon his hat,
Sparkling icicles
Dangling from the edge.
The snowman's face
As bright as the moon.
Soon the sun
Will come out from behind the clouds
And the snowman will turn into a puddle.

Laura Hay (9)
Furze Platt Junior School

HOPE

Hope is a bright and light blue,
She smells like brand new flowers,
She tastes like melted chocolate,
She sounds like a little bird.
Hope has the fur of a cat.
Hope lives in a force field of goodness.

Colin Cooper (10)
Furze Platt Junior School

HOPE

Hope is the colour of baby pink,
It smells like new spring flowers.
Hope tastes like melted chocolate,
It sounds like spring birds singing.
Hope feels like a smooth cloth
And lives in a forest of beautiful flowers.

Morgan Smith (10)
Furze Platt Junior School

UNHAPPINESS

Unhappiness is jet-black,
It smells like old, burnt coal.
Unhappiness tastes sour and mouldy,
It sounds like a gunfire.
It feels as sharp as a knife.
Unhappiness lives in the deepest, darkest jungle.

Abigail Giles (10)
Furze Platt Junior School

DEATH

Death is a mix of grey, black and green,
It smells like rotting bones and blood,
It tastes as if you were dead,
It whistles through the air like a deadly ghost,
It flies past you and gives a sudden cold feeling,
It lives in the grave.

Thomas Hopkins (10)
Furze Platt Junior School

WAR

War is black,
It smells like smoke,
It tastes like poison,
It sounds like gunshots,
It feels like lava,
It lives in *Hell.*

Tim Armstrong (9)
Furze Platt Junior School

DEATH

Death is the colour of the black sky at night
And smells like the yolk of a rotten egg.
It tastes like black, dried blood
And sounds like a muffled zombie.
It feels like the skin of a warty toad
And lives in the darkness of my loft.

Sam Langford (10)
Furze Platt Junior School

HOPE

Hope is silver,
It smells like chocolate cooking,
And tastes like strawberries,
It sounds like birds singing,
And feels like petals from a flower,
Hope lives in the summer sun.

Amelia Hilsdon (10)
Furze Platt Junior School

NASTINESS

Nastiness is black,
It smells like poisonous petrol fumes.
Nastiness tastes of charcoal and is gritty,
It sounds like nails on a blackboard,
It feels strong and painful.
Nastiness lives in a pirate's grave.

Thomas Davies (10)
Furze Platt Junior School

ILLNESS

Illness is a pale peach colour,
It smells like strong cough medicine.
Illness tastes like salty sea water,
It sounds like ill birds chirping.
Illness feels mushy and gooey,
It lives in the heart of rotten foods.

Grace Grimmett (10)
Furze Platt Junior School

DISEASE

Disease is a slimy green
And it smells like rotting bodies.
It tastes like a red-hot branding iron,
It has the sound of a screaming child.
Disease feels like a ghostly slime,
It lives in the burning war field.

Richard Dean (9)
Furze Platt Junior School

WORLD WAR II

They were overjoyed,
They were so thrilled,
They went together
To be wedded.

The bridesmaid's gown,
The page boy's suit,
They paid them back
With lots of loot.

The air raid sound,
The bombs did come,
The man he was
A widower.

The man said, 'Oh,
Oh, woe is me
My new wedded wife
Is gone from me.'

The air raid sound,
The bombs did come,
The house was
The only thing left.

The air raid sound,
The bombs did come,
The house was not,
Then there was none.

Henry Stone (10)
Furze Platt Junior School

COLD

Cold is dark blue,
It smells like burning rubber,
It tastes like mouldy potatoes,
It sounds like a police siren,
It feels like slimy gunk,
It lives in the core of the world.

Christopher Hopkins (10)
Furze Platt Junior School

HAPPINESS

Happiness is yellow,
It smells like fresh strawberries,
It tastes like chocolate ice cream,
It sounds like children playing,
It feels like rippling water.
Happiness lives in your heart.

Gregory Smith (9)
Furze Platt Junior School

DISAPPOINTMENT

Disappointment is dark blue
It smells like horrible seaweed
Disappointment tastes cold and salty
It sounds like the roaring sea
It feels sharp and gritty
Disappointment lives at the bottom of the sea.

Victoria Gravestock (10)
Furze Platt Junior School

WAR

War is as black as a night
War smells like burnt toast
War tastes like black pepper
War sounds like fire burning
War feels like a death trap
War lives in the evil soul.

Craig Deane (9)
Furze Platt Junior School

DEATH

Death is pitch-black
It smells like gas pushing through your nostrils
It tastes like rotten poison sizzling on your tongue
It sounds like screams from every direction
It feels like walking through blazing hot fire
It lives at the bottom of the dark underworld.

Clementine Tissier (9)
Furze Platt Junior School

HOPE

Hope is the colour of pearly pink
It smells like a cake that's just come out the oven
It tastes like smooth strawberries
It sounds like a lullaby
It feels soft and smooth
Hope lives inside you.

Victoria Binns (9)
Furze Platt Junior School

DEATH

Death is black
It smells like decaying bodies
It tastes like polluted water
It sounds like thunder
It feels like emptiness
It lives in the skull of a vulture.

Thomas Clark (10)
Furze Platt Junior School

HOPE

Hope is light turquoise
It smells like fresh air and flowers
Hope tastes of fizzy sherbet
It sounds like birds singing
It feels soft, warm and bouncy
Hope lives at the edge of the heart.

Alice Marshall (9)
Furze Platt Junior School

HOPE

Hope is such a pale pink
It smells as sweet as perfume
It tastes as nice as strawberries
It sounds like a lullaby
It feels soft and warm
Hope lives in your heart.

Emma Runesson (9)
Furze Platt Junior School

FALCON

The falcon flies like the wind,
Stares at me, glares at me.
Sounds as silent as a rat,
Hunts the prey better than cats.
But when it flies very, very high
It is surely time to say 'Goodbye'.

Matthew Bowles (10)
Furze Platt Junior School

FEAR

Fear is a very pale green,
With the smell of sweat,
And the taste of illness,
It sounds like bad music,
And it feels like guilt.
It lives with the Devil, down in Hell.

Laura Haworth (9)
Furze Platt Junior School

ANGER

Anger is blood-red
It smells like burning scraps of iron
Anger tastes like poison
It sounds like a volcano erupting
It feels like it's burning your hands
Anger lives in red-hot fire.

Emma Kettley (10)
Furze Platt Junior School

HOPE

Hope is a bright, light blue
It smells like a piece of fresh air
Hope tastes like a crisp, chocolate cake
It sounds like a peaceful bird singing
Hope feels like a silken piece of velvet
It lives on the very top of your heart.

Sean Fraser (10)
Furze Platt Junior School

MADNESS

Madness is purple and lime green
It smells like rotten bananas
It tastes tangy and then mouldy
It sounds like a forgotten spirit
It feels like an electric eel
It lives in an old tramp's rags.

Alex Clark (10)
Furze Platt Junior School

ANGRY WORDS HURT LIKE . . .

A long snake coiling round my friendship
Fiery flames burning my thoughts
Queen wasps stinging my mind so I can't think.
A sharp pencil poking into my happiness
A stingray stinging my thoughts
Chilli sauce burning my tongue so I can't speak
A dagger piercing my concentration.

Finlay Donaldson (9)
Herries Preparatory School

ANGRY WORDS HURT LIKE . . .

A long, long snake bite
A venomous snake bite
Into your now bleeding heart
Thoughts of it won't go away
Like the bite over and over again
Repeating what hurt you so much
Your heart keeps bleeding rapidly
And there's nothing you can do about it.

George Santa-Olalla (9)
Herries Preparatory School

ANGRY WORDS HURT LIKE . . .

A lethal wasp sting right in my nerves,
An icy freeze burn cutting into my thoughts,
Someone painfully punching me,
A scissor stab right into my heart,
An arrow straight into my soul.

Richard Stafford (8)
Herries Preparatory School

ROLLER COASTER

The roller
The roller coaster
We're going really fast
How long's it going to last?

Mum shivers
Dad quivers
I scream
Aaaaah!

Mum's sick
The roller coaster's too slick
We're at the end
Mum's going round the bend
Dad's gone barmy
I want a sarnie.

Katy Gibson (8)
Highfield School

HANDS

Dirty hands,
Clean hands,
Sticky hands,
Smooth hands,
Bony hands,
Thick hands, freckled hands,
And ones with bitten nails.

Working hands,
Lazy hands,
Tired hands,
Dancing hands,
Stiff hands
And one's that make shadows on the wall.

They pick things up,
They put things down,
The wiggle, they fiddle,
They move all around,
They bump,
They jump,
They clap,
They slap,
They push,
They handle things and touch.

Kate Horne (10)
Highfield School

HENRY THE 8TH

Henry the 8th,
He smelt like an ape,
And ate a lot of bananas,

He had six wives,
And ruined their lives,
He had them all murdered inside his castle,

He loved to fight,
You should have seen the sight,
When he flicked his servants' eyes out,

But when he died,
What a great surprise,
They held an enormous party!

Charlotte Wiggins (10)
Highfield School

- OR WHAT ABOUT THIS?

I'm thinking of a poem,
I don't know what about,
It's for a competition,
Ideas are going in and out.

I could do one about pirates,
I read one in a book,
They had a tattoo of . . . money bags,
The captain had a hook.

Although I could write one about the weather,
How it rains every day,
Or one about kitchens,
I won't win with that - no way.

What about a poem with a rabbit,
All white and fluffy,
Or what about this one?
It's great, it's cool, it's 'Buffy'!

- Hang on, this could be my poem,
I have a chance to win,
Then again I might not,
It's going in the bin!

Alex Snell (11)
Highfield School

MY GUINEA PIG

My guinea pig is brown and white all over,
He loves the smell of fresh, green clover,
He loves to hide in the hay,
And sometimes he stays there all the day.

My guinea pig's tongue is small and pink,
And it often makes me think,
Of how a creature so tiny and small
Can roll its body into a ball.

My guinea pig loves to run around,
And he often rolls along the ground,
He munches and crunches on his hay,
He does it in a funny way.

My guinea pig rolls around on my lap,
And always gets into a flap.

From this poem you can see,
I love my guinea pig
And he loves me.

Gabrielle Allen (10)
Highfield School

MY CAT

I've got a cat,
All white and black,
He's not a fat cat,
I'm sure of that!

Hector is his name,
Eating is his game,
He walks around,
Not making a sound.

His eyes are green,
And he keeps himself clean.
He's my favourite cat,
And he knows that!

Annabel Charan Banks (10)
Highfield School

THE ALIEN

When the alien arrived on my street
We really were surprised
There were remarks like
'Freaky' 'Funny' 'Weird' 'Wacky'
We asked him in and this is what he replied
'My name is Thawackymakeybakysaky
and I would like to come in.'

When the alien arrived on my street
We really were surprised
When he came in we asked him if he wanted a fry-up
And he replied
'My name is Thawackymakeybakysaky
and I would like a fry-up.'

When the alien arrived on my street
We really were surprised
After he'd finished we asked him whether he'd like to sleep
in the spare room
And this is what he replied
'My name is Thawackymakeybakysaky
and I would like to sleep in the spare room.'

Suzannah Bridge (10)
Highfield School

SCHOOL DINNERS

If you stay to school dinners,
And you know what they're like.
Then listen to me,
Because you know I'm right.

You *know* you should eat them,
But who cares!
They taste revolting,
And give you the scares.

If you eat them,
Without a doubt.
You'll soon know
What I'm on about.

For when you get home,
The very same night.
You'll be sick down the loo,
And give your mum a fright.

So now you know,
The dreadful fate,
Of those poor kids,
Who stay until late.

Aimée Campbell (10)
Highfield School

LITTLE BUBBLE

Out of a coloured pot you came
Yellow, Orange, Blue,
I'm the one who blew on you,
So therefore I created you!

Soft and shiny, round and fat,
Little bubble floating free
Over the top of me.
Different shapes and sizes too
When I huff and puff on you!

Then suddenly you float slower,
And gradually get smaller.
Oh no! I cry
Oh! Not my bubble!
Now, I'll have to blow another!

Holly Chapman (11)
Highfield School

THE LAST WORDS MY FATHER SAID!

The last words my father said,
When I visited him in the hospital bed,
One unusually sunny day.
He squinted at me, I moved nearer his way,
The heat of the day rather took my breath away.
My dream, I never knew or saw,
To sail the sea and to explore,
Oh to stay on this earth one day more.
I stared at him
He stared back
Beep! Beep! Beep! Beep! I stumbled back.
He had a bad medical
Attack
And he was dead.
I kissed his grey and wrinkly head
And I walked away.

Elizabeth Fox (10)
Highfield School

GYMNASTICS!

I hate gymnastics,
They're really quite a bore,
Let's try and do a back-flip,
I end up on the floor!

I hate gymnastics,
All the warming up and stuff,
All the bending and stretching,
I would rather wear ear muffs!

I hate gymnastics,
I can only do a roly-poly - just,
I'll try and do a cartwheel,
But only if I must!

I hate gymnastics,
Well, they're okay,
I'm getting more interested,
I now go every Saturday!

Lucy Fredericks (10)
Highfield School

TITANIC

The cold, wet wind was blowing, people were screaming,
The funnel was beaming,
Women crying to see their husbands, but they are probably dead,
Children wishing they were in their bed.
The lifeboats are disappearing into the middle of the night,
The moon had gone, there was no more light,
The funnel crashes down, water spraying everywhere.
Everyone watches as the Titanic sinks slowly down,
The freezing cold water was killing the people in the sea.
The lifeboats return only to hear the silence of death.

Helene Green (11)
Highfield School

CHOCOLATE FACTORY BOY

There was a boy who loved to eat a rather unhealthy food,
It gave him something very smelly and quite unpleasantly rude,
He saved up all his pocket money so he could buy his dream.
To go to a great sized chocolate factory, I hope there is ice cream!
He pleaded and pleaded to his mum, to go,
'If you come back you'll be as fat as a marshmallow'
Then he went to his dad in a loving way and said
'Would you come and play and let me have a dream come true,
Oh come on Dad, I do love you.'

Emma Alington (9)
Highfield School

TEMPTATION OF A CHOCOLATE CAKE

Cakes are yummy and scrummy in my tummy,
Like this one downstairs.
It's piled in metres and metres,
And its thick chocolate layers are melting.
Shall I go and get it?
Or stay here in temptation,
Suffer such temptation.
But it's my sister's,
Oh well! Who cares?
She would eat my chocolate cake,
So I will eat hers.
It's crying my name as I creep downstairs,
Now I will count to three,
And it will all be gone in one.
1 . . . 2 . . . 3
Yum! Yum! Yum!
It's in my tum,
I hope my sister won't mind.

Amy Calcott (9)
Highfield School

MY CATS

My cats are black and white,
Kittens they are,
You'll love them at first sight.

They both have marble eyes,
And are sweet and fluffy too,
I hope you'll love them
Because *I do!*

Lauren Curtis (9)
Highfield School

MY CAT

She isn't black,
She isn't white,
But I think my cat is just right.

She isn't thin,
She isn't fat,
But I think cats are nice like that.

She isn't big,
She isn't small,
But I think she's the best of all!

Charlotte Fuscone (10)
Highfield School

MY CATS

My cats Chelsea and Forest.
They mix rather well.
One is tortoiseshell and short-haired
And one just plain grey.

Chelsea is very fluffy,
Very lazy too.
Forest is very playful
And always wanting *food!*

Harriett Ingall (10)
Highfield School

THINGS I HEAR AND SEE

Bees go buzz,
Slides go squeak,
The little, poor dogs are just so weak.
Lollipops just go whirl, whirl, whirl.
I can hear a girl munching on a Twirl.
The ducks and geese are playing around,
Chittering, chattering on the ground,
The little babies are looking around,
Seeing if the treasure was found.
There is a couple sitting down,
The man is pretending to be a clown.
I wonder where my Mother's gone,
She's probably lying in the sun,
Perhaps I will go and lie down,
And dream about what I've seen today.

Bethany John (10)
Highfield School

THE SWAN

The swan glides gracefully through the lake,
Its feathers are pearl-white like the snow.
Her amber beak dips in and out,
Looking about for food.

Emily Law (10)
Highfield School

MY SHADOW

My shadow is deep black,
Sometimes deep, deep, grey,
Following me every moment,
In the night, in the day.

When the sun is shining,
Brightly in the sky,
My shadow is behind or ahead,
Or anywhere nearby.

It follows me down the road,
It follows me round the bend,
It follows me anywhere else,
My shadow is my friend.

Samantha Riley (10)
Highfield School

IT'S NOT FAIR!

It's not fair,
My sister's allowed
To have her radio turned up loud.

It's not fair,
She's always at the cinema,
She's allowed to sit
In the front of the car.

It's not fair,
My sister stays up
Really late,
To sit and daze.

I know she is older than me,
So I suppose it's fair
Don't you see?

Olivia Shepherd (9)
Highfield School

ANCIENT TREASURES

Ancient treasures beneath the ground
Not moving nor stirring, not making a sound
The treasures of Pompeii they lie and wait
Their magic will have gone if we uncover them too late.

Inspiring mosaics which were once walked on
But the owners are now dead and gone
Some jewellery, a bowl, a pot and a pan
All held onto by a time-frozen man.

Vesuvius now lies quiet and still
A gentle, unsmoking, rock-hard hill
Once, long ago, it sprang into fire
The flames shot high but the smoke rose higher.

The ash covered the ground in a huge, thick layer
People and possessions are still there
Nobody lived, they all are dead
Sleeping beneath the lava bed.

Imogen Ash (9)
Highfield School

MY TWO BROTHERS

I went to the swimming pool with my two brothers
It was really fun
First we had a race but guess who won?
Joe, Joe, Joe.

Then we all jumped in together to see who could stay down the longest
Joe gave a flick, Nick gave a kick
But guess who popped up first?
Me, then Joe
We both waited a second and then came a kick
So guess who won?
Nick, Nick, Nick.

It was time to go
Time to have tea
We all went together, we three.

After tea it was time to go home
So it would be just me and my mummy
All alone.

Amy Cooper (8)
Highfield School

MY CAT

I've got a cat who wears a hat
Her name is Pat and she sits on the mat.

When she is happy she purrs
So much so, she never stirs.

So often at home I will stay
So that with Pat I can play.

When I give her food to eat
She quickly jumps to her feet.

After her food she jumps on my lap
And lies down to enjoy a cat nap.

Natasha Cross (8)
Highfield School

Going To Bed

Going to bed is a boring idea,
All the grown-ups stay up, go to pubs and drink beer.
I don't see why we have to rest,
I think that staying up should be the best!
If you stay up you'll have more time to play,
You could have midnight feasts every day!
After all, beds are such hard work to make,
I suppose you could sleep in the bath, but for heaven's sake,
Why should sleeping be our daily routine,
When it's that time - I'm not too keen.
It's not to stop you getting thin,
Okay, so it's to care for your skin.
But then, why can't you just always wash?
Every day until we're looking posh.
Why do we have such astonishing dreams?
It is quite bizarre to us, or so it seems.

Jennifer Firman (9)
Highfield School

THE HARRIS HAWK

The Harris hawk is black all round,
When soaring he does not make a sound,
And when his deadly claws show,
He grasps his prey and flies away.

His sharp, curved beak eats the prey,
While his beady eyes show the way,
And his chestnut shoulders stand out bold,
As he flies away throughout the day.

Rebecca Law (8)
Highfield School

MY BOAT

My boat sails on the rough, blue sea
The wind blows in my hair
The seagulls squawk in the wild wind
As if they don't really care.

The dolphins jump in and out of the rough, blue sea
In the golden sun it shines on me
My boat rocks like a rocking horse going very fast
The sails flap like a birds wing in the golden, blue sky.

Nathalie Miller (8)
Highfield School

THE UNICORNS

In the heart of many forests, far from man's eyes,
A thunder of hooves beneath the fresh, blue skies,
Tells us the unicorns roam, the hunter dies.

The shining, golden, ribboned horn,
The hunter's T-shirt that is torn
The unicorns playing until dawn.

The mythical creature that is so rare,
Only would an evil person dare
To glance at it with a piercing stare.

The unicorns cry that is like a neigh
May all peace rest in hay
But unicorns cannot stay.

This is when evil is known
It is like a quilted blanket that is sewn
With great care and not a moan.

The unicorns do believe
That they retrieve
Nothing that is naive.

Emma Wilkinson (8)
Highfield School

LITTLE ROBIN REDBREAST

Little robin redbreast
Makes himself a little nest
Where he takes his winter rest.

There he merrily chirps
On the leafless birch
Which is his favourite perch.

Alice Winson (9)
Highfield School